SIGNALS OF
SMOKE AND ASH

SIGNALS OF
SMOKE AND ASH

Evan Quitelle

ISBN: 978-1-4669-0394-4 (sc)
ISBN: 978-1-4669-0395-1 (hc)
ISBN: 978-1-4669-0396-8 (e)

Library of Congress Control Number: 2011960292

Trafford rev. 11/07/2011

 www.trafford.com

North America & International
toll-free: 1 888 232 4444 (USA & Canada)
phone: 250 383 6864 ♦ fax: 812 355 4082

Contents

Also by Evan Quitelle "Indian Summer"

Photography by Evan Quitelle

This Book is dedicated to

Linwood and Marlene

To the

Wroten's and the Brockington's

Acknowledgements

JCUR1ST. To Angela Lewis, Qari Dontrelle, Briel Aleja, Kendrick Larenz, Kendra Lanai, Aylisha Marquetta and Aunj^sheline. Special thanks to Jacqueline Rhodes, Kelvin McGhee, Serene Hutcherson and Linwood Wroten (my Halo). To Anjelah Louis and to my fellow poets Adriann (The Pen) Bautista and Michela Wolfe McGhee. To the love of my life Lavender Black.

Carmelita,

May God richly bless and bless and bless you.

Your friend

The Angel of Saint Evan's Parish

Ardor is the sconce
an angel provoking light
now I have vision

Dwelling on The Past

I miss the water near Yesterday
how we drank with laughter
and you taking a dip

I miss the wilderness with wild honey
how I borrowed from you and
you paying me back

I miss coming down
off of our high horse and
casting shadows on the sundial

I miss our native tongues
your cardinal points and
filling the feel of you

I miss standing just
outside the frame
digging your scene

I miss captured in brief
laced hips and satin lips
pursed for satisfaction

I miss the pilgrimage south
the middle passage how you
compass rose and I nourished the bloom

I miss you breaking the fall
when I reached out and
I held on to holding you

And Rain

Walking along the
chocolate sands
of the ocean floor
holding hands
filling the cerulean gap
disrobed from
the weight of waiting
I want to feel your hands
undoing the best of me
then tying me all in knots
there are only two things
I love more
filling the
cerulean gap
calligraphy
the beautiful
writing of
the pen
and rain

The Bells

The clouds in her eyes
began a down pour
the petals from the trees
were white like snow
as they took flight in the wind
a Philadelphia rain was in the air
and it was the palsy that caused
another crack in the belle

Taxiing the Runway

Momentum is building
not quite ready to take flight
but soon all things will be soar
she is going to recline
decline things on ice
her life is more than just peanuts
she is the pilot of her destiny
on the verge of being great
with her feet firmly on the ground
the turtle's dove is about to take heir

Rain Check

Pushing her hips out the door
was necessary otherwise
the dialogue between us
would have been in tongues
if she had any intentions of
letting out her sails and if my
honorable intentions were meant
to soar then I had to watch
those curves take the door

The Foundations of Her

She gave me an hourglass
so that I would have her time
I planted a seed between
child bearing hips
so that she could give
birth to love
upon bedclothes
just exposed
her foundations were laid
juxtapose

Pardon My Reach for Heaven

When you sold Girl Scout cookies
and I collected merit badges
when I played tee ball and
you wore that funny looking tutu
that made you itch when you
were still daddy's little girl and he
would bounce with you on the see saw
when I rode the shoulders of my father
and gave piggy back rides to sister
when you were a tomboy following
your big brother around and I was
doing what boys do when you became
rebellious and I made the team
I did not want to hold your hand
I wanted to hold your attention

Nursing Her Home

She is jealous of the pen
she is jealous of the serene moments
she is jealous of just the right shoe
jealous of Clif the twig and Bet
she is jealous of the Basileus
jealous of the stethoscope
that hears my heart beat
of my funny bone because it
is able to make me smile
all this jealousy makes her crazy
and I am jealous of the padded
walls that circumscribes her

Amethyst Junction

She is the birth of a flower and I am committed to her bloom
I am committed to the butterfly even while she is in her cocoon
I am committed to her clouds because surely she is high enough to reign
I am committed to the chameleon though her season is apt to change
I am committed to healing I know it is only a bruise
I am committed to cerulean, indigo and all shades of her blues
I am committed to the scars they are her marks of beauty
I am committed to watering her fields for I am a duty
I am committed to the groundhog leaving her without a shadow of doubt
I am committed to Brie oh to see her ripen so devout
I am committed to the heart I am her word of function
I am committed to Lavender for she is the amethyst junction
I am committed to the mirror image for it is a reflection of her
I am the cypress knee in Eden committing to the gardener

Thorns in the Nest of Egos

In relations to golf
a hole in one
is a shot from the tee
eagle is two under par
birdie is one under par
par for the course
starts with foreplay
and since you refuse to stroke my ego
you are unable to come
enjoy the waterfalls of Heaven

Blindfolds

What good is a blindfold
if I have tunnel vision
and your thigh casts
a shadow on the light
at the end
obstructing my rearview
my only option is to
light a peripheral fire
causing you to consider
my point of view

Down To the Gristle

I love your smile
your sultry style
the way you walk
that country mile

love your full moon
your exit in June
the way you come
not a minute too soon

I love your eclipse
your scarlet hips
from your toes
to your finger tips

She Loves Me Knot

I sent her flowers
with a lavender bow
but perhaps there was
not enough sunlight
perhaps not enough
nourishment
maybe I did not water
enough
maybe I should have
communicated better
and given a cause
to take root
because just like
the relationship
the flowers died

Clouded

There is a wolf in the sky
I know that you see it as a cloud
but there is definitely a wolf
its bark is like thunder and its
bite is lightning
beware this is no time to sleep
beware do not count this wolf as sheep

Raindrops for Synthetic Roses

The greenhouse is not serving its purpose
all life has withered and died
what do we do with things that no longer
have a purpose
if we tear it down then where will we go
when we want to plant a seed
where will we go when
love is in bloom
and there is a need to nourish the flame
what do we do with raindrops
when life is a synthetic rose

Tender Ness

The bed is tattered and torn
from years of abuse
should have been replaced long ago
too much sleeping going on
and not enough embrace
sometimes a bed is meant for
more than just sleep
sometimes it is meant for
lavender and lilies
sometimes it is meant
to plant tenderness

Fills Me

Second class citizen Wednesday is
she is middle of the week
she is not my beginning or my end
she is my journey half full
she is a blessing she has healing power
I have gladly traded all of my flock
just to elevate on Wednesday
because she makes the middle weak

The Duke of Diamond Street

Pink Champale on poker nights
right after the kids were all tuckered
from playing king ball where I ruled
or jacks and double Dutch and
Chinese Jump rope and hoops
on milk crates and tops in the
streets and mother may I
go outside because the girl
next door has blossomed and
I have my first Italian ice crush
and I want to share my last
now and later

The Truth Naked

I want the truth naked
down to the gristle
like in the garden
before the serpent
when even the tortoise
relinquished its refuge
I want bared souls
and hearts in the wilderness
let your cloak fall to the earth
and become dust
show me your freedom
you say with confidence
that you desire to be elevated
let go of the things
that are holding you down
let go of your waits and soar

Check Mate

I have longed to be above it all
or as calm as the ocean floor
I want to have the advantage on Venus
at love to serve in her court
and I will be
every day the knight for my queen
as she holds me captive

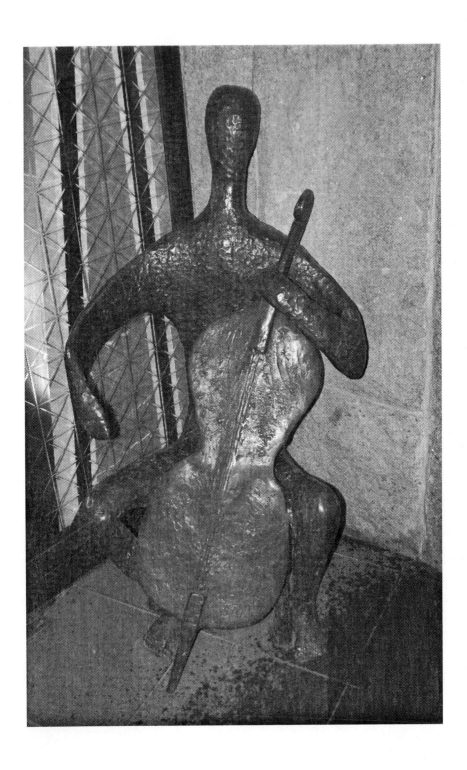

Pecan Parmesan Crusted Rainbow Love

Imagine the rainflower
refusing to bloom
then you will understand
why I no longer want
to remain friends

love has blossomed

Dancing To the Awkward Silence

There is
a woman
that has
never seen
the rain

no matter
how she
dances she
is unable
to stir
the waves

there is
a trial
in tribulation
desert

no matter
the volume
of her
frequency

Tropical Depression

Even
the
horizon
longs
to
be
sipping
on
a
sunrise
sunset
replacing
strawberries
with
kiwi

An Acquired Taste

To
survive
in
the
trenches
when
love
is
the
only
ration
you
must
savor
every
morsel

when
there
is
no
surrender
you
will
find
flavor
in
the
retreat

Objects in the Mirror Are Closer Than They Appear

When
the
object
of
my
affection
is
far
away

I
look
for
a
reflection
of
herself

U-N-I-Verse

Words

can
not
explain
how
I
just
want
it
to
be
you
and
I
pair
a
phrasing
this
world
but
you
belong
to
the
universe

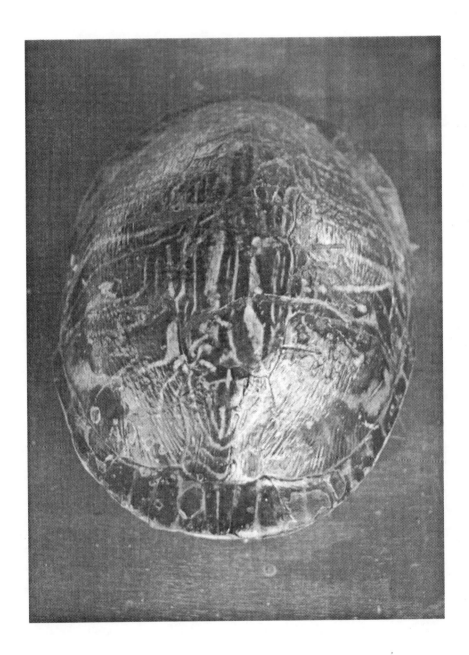

Rainbow Harvest

Every
day
is
a
new
color

yesterday
was
black
and
white
embellished
in
teal
but
today
is
blue
and
voluptuous
lime
softly
caressing
chocolate
diamonds
and
buttermilk
buns

Write As Rain

If you were here
there would be thunder in the backyard
and things would be all wet

if you were here
there would be puddles to splash in
and pockets would be plenty

if you were here
there'd be promises of rainbows
and we'd spoon after soup and sandwiches

if you were here
life would be poetry
and it would be write as rain

Lily in Bloom

I
appreciate
you

Lady
I
Love
You

how
your
perfume
lingers
and
permeates
my
world
you
are
my
rain
flower
you
make
my
words
beautiful

The Good Crystal

I want to save
the good crystal
I wish that every day
could be that special
I want to sit by
the window and watch
the rain forever
to savor every drop
I want to confess
to her my sins
how I dipped my quill
into too much ink
and tattooed my words
across too many pages
I want to save
the good crystal
and on the next occasion
she can save me

Black Lavender

I travel at the speed of dark
and you are the light
that keeps up with me

I am cooled in the deepest shade
but you are the color
that permeates my soul

I am midnight
intoxicated by
your moon shine

I am a black butterfly
happy to be dancing
in a field of lavender

I am a dark continent
that thinks the world of
you

Life inside the Tortoise Shell

Even the iridescent butterfly had to cocoon
and the chameleon has to adapt to change
the mantis believes in prayer and
even though it is a tangled web to weave
the black widow dines on love
the moth in its burning desire thirsts for the flame
and upon hearing the music the worms dig the groove
the ants take to the hills and
the frogs have taken a leap of faith
but my life is spent inside the tortoise shell
taking up refuge with you

A Serene Moment

I yelled stop to the wind as if I had the power
for some reason it stopped and started again
mocking me as if to say did you forget your place
it is not your arms that are too short but your legs
not long enough to keep step to the cadence of love
life was serene for a moment but I continued to sing
off key there is no perfect melody under the sun
so I aspire to put its shine under my feet

A Mahogany Still

French manicured fingernails attached to dainty hands
the extension of a skinny arm rested on the curve of her hips
her elbow brushed against me as I attempted to squeeze past
down the crowded Market Street I stopped a mahogany still
as I eyed the outfit a moss green and then I noticed that in the
reflection in the store front window she wore nothing but a halo
and sage eyes and as I turned to glance she was more beautiful
than the reflection and I imagined her in the outfit from the window
at a restaurant overlooking the harbor where a clock ceased
to keep time in between heart beats and breaths on hiatus

Do It Faux Love

You collagen
you thin thin
too constant
you implant
you nip and tuck
you liposuck
you quest bigger bun
you sensational no. 1
you yaky
you remy
roots do dye
chameleon eye
you nose tweak
to change the peak
to perk them up
you double cup
you enhance
for circumstance
purse your lips
acrylic tips
you smaller box
you Botox
decrease you mass
you by pass
the sag the shift
the drift you lift
you beauty diminish
as you faux finish

Faithful

I will be faithful to Lily
even when she's not in bloom
faithful to the butterfly
while still in her cocoon
faithful to the bluebird
as she makes her nest
faithful to the tide because
she always returns to shore
to the sky because even when I am lost
in the wilderness she never leaves me
to the mountain that sits to the
north after standing the test of time
at some point she reaches her peak
faithful to the lightning because
like a pugilist she strikes back
faithful to the bell
she is not afraid to take toll
faithful to the sundial
she counts every second blessed
faithful to the mayfly for in
one day she enjoys a lifespan
faithful to the second wind
she just blows me away
to the oak tree she knows to take root
to the stoic river for a period
of time she stands still
faithful to the lavender angel
as she ascends to the clouds
for surely she is purple reign

Good Mourning

The night trembles
it is nervous about
coming to an end
it has been draped
in thick pleasure and
fondled with regret
as the morning escapes
from the clouds and
the night begins to die
will we remember
the mount of yesterday
what we had to lie down
to take our stand

Speak Easy

Sippin on an ultra violet light
intoxicated by the spirits
that excites electrons
refusing to let the bottom of the glass go
drunk from her night and her day
from her tequila sunrise to moon shine
soberly it is the medicine pre scribed
the intonation of her pen her ink
speaks in volumes it is nectar from the tap
in verse it is liqueur from her lips
her rhetoric is foreplay her dialogue seduces
her soliloquy ties me in knots
and then kissed by her words
going down easy I come
undone

Puddles

Puddles don't run deep enough
to consider the swim up stream
or to draw your waters from
or to make your wishing well
don't pan for gold in puddles
the only joy is in the splash
which lasts a fleeting moment
but when boots are unlaced
the same goes for pockets

How to Make Blue

Today I saw your glow
and you shine like the yellow
rays of sun and I play it cool
like the tall sleek blades of green pasture
reaching for your nourishment
and when we consummate . . . .

. . . . blue skies

Delicious in Dance

If you choose to chaise
and stay a while
then you will invite the
rhapsody
if you allow me to catch you firefly
and leave you ajar
I will not allow you to die verse
if you permit me to come inside
from the rain I will be a refuge
if you are delicious in dance
and velvet procrastination
and when turned inside out
your beauty still calendars
if I love the things that
I do not like about you
if you are indigenous to indigo
or the lavender blush
then my borders are the Agape Sea

Write All the Wrongs

She complained about things being off the hinge
she complained about things broken
complained about the squeak
complained about the leak
about the crack
about the drip
the hole
the draught
my pen
ignited a fire that fixed them all
now her only complaint is the fire

Uncle

Has a drawer for everything
everything is neatly tucked
there is a drawer for all the utensils
a mean nothing is run amuck
he has a drawer for all the spices of life
there is even a drawer for the scrapple knife
a drawer if you need to scale back
scissor shear cut or prune
there is a drawer for the potholders
the pan handles and even the silver spoon
a drawer for the matches to start the flame
he has a place for any and everything you name
a hammer drawer and even a drawer for rubber gloves
I once asked Uncle where I'd find love
he replied it's in the drawer labeled survival
that is where I keep
The Holy Bible

I the Storm

I figured it out and now I am the martyr
tomorrow speaks in tongues about a future
that promises its own existence if I bless it
there is power in my healing so I chose to give
you and you power to blow to embrace
the second wind I have married wisdom
in a beautiful celestial ceremony overlooking
the as far as the eye can sea and what has been
joined cannot be put asunder so scriptures strike
with words that read like thunder and assail the seas
and I am the sailor and the vessel I the storm am calm
taking toll for the belle so loud that it can still be heard
in December so indelible that it seeps through to the soul
in a dialect so delectable that if you feast on my words you
will never dine alone

Blue You a Kiss

Tracing the outline
of lips so full
while being caressed
by the dark
I remember your words
through ink
stains pressed gently
against
my finger tips that returned
to my own
and held there in suspended
animation
and you painting the air
with strokes of blue
the touch of the gentle wind
posing as you

Turning Iraq Around

It is a task trying to find your place on the map
at times when things are black
when the path is dim
when comes a whirlwind

on the path to becoming
you need direction
when things look slim
your sails are not trim

at times when things are topside down
and going is the wrong way
loosen the cape
crawl through the wake

remember you are here
and like the river
that flows through be centered
be it stern be stout

come about

Anyes

While miracles were being
performed on aisle seven
to victims of the rainbow
I was building a nest
in the curve of her hips
as she proceeded beyond
my heart to touch the soul
there was pleasure in her smile
in her walk there was
a sashay full of dreams
her kisses were comfort
food in the sleepy zone
and forever she went

abducting the crowd

Conversations with the Clif

Some dangling participles are from a twig
sharp witted conspiracy and me the person
in this place amongst these things
I have been modified
in theory
I listened astutely and deciphered the message
when most saw it as a gamble
I learned to hold the right cards
and even in the folly
I still understood the wisdom

When The Chip Is Down
There Is a Blessing Coming Up

Standing in the pulpit you see a man before you
looking regal in a tailor made suit his shirt is lightly
starched and crisp wearing a silk tie and Italian leather
shoes with manicured nails he is well groomed and
dressed to the nines and if you look closely you will
notice that he is wearing shiny monogrammed cufflinks
but what you may not know is that under that tailor
made suit are the ashiest knees ever I know that
the congregation's inclination is to offer lotion but
no thanks because if you get hung up on the lotion
you will miss the fact that there is already an anointing

there is pride in the ash there is inheritance from the ash
this man's mother and grandmother had those same ashy
knees you see they spent a lot of time down on their knees
looking up and their offspring their survivors got blessed
think of Noah building an ark of gopher wood surely he was ashy
and the survivors receiving the inheritance were three sons begot
had Lot took time to concern himself with the ash from Sodom
and Gomorrah to dust it off he too would have looked back but
survivors his daughters came out from the ash to receive inheritance
Jesus the carpenter ashy hands in the wilderness on his knees
for forty days and forty nights anointed and blessed who are his
survivors who receives the inheritance his children
and we celebrate on the anniversary of his resurrection

clips from the anniversary of the attack on the towers
is about the firemen and the survivors of the ash
the anniversary of the earthquakes in Haiti depicts
how those that survived the ruble and ash were blessed
the survivors of the tsunami in Japan salvaged
what came out of the ruble and ash
anyone that has ever been through the fire knows how
precious it is to salvage something that has survived the ash
an anniversary is about the survivor and their inheritance
the congregation has this inheritance the man before you
has this inheritance he doesn't concern himself with the ash
he is a survivor of the ash he has the anointing
and when he is down on his knees in prayer
when the Chip is down there is a blessing coming up

The High Priestess

She stopped believing
in Santa Claus
and the Tooth Fairy
a long time ago
she doesn't believe in gambling
doesn't believe in war
she doesn't believe that marriage is
a fairy tale or is always a happy ending
she doesn't believe in voodoo
doesn't believe in ghost
she doesn't believe in
witchcraft or black magic
doesn't believe in Friday the 13th,
black cats or other superstitions
she is the high priestess

. . . and she believes in me

Placing Bet's

Sometimes we stop to get
a pretzel when we are
exhausted from visiting all
the stores

most times things are
done in reverse and
then we start all over
again

always we create
memories that last way
past the expiration of
the sale

Even the River Bends in Prayer

There were shades of pink
glistening atop the river
from the rainbow
and the sound of the water in praise
basking in the presence of God
and there she was the river
looking like an angel
and the fuchsia rainbow her halo
getting wet with words of affirmation
and like the ornaments of her request
the river encompassed a large territory
and its sashay kept on blessing
like the angel's flow

Evan Quitelle

Mauvelous

Our foundation is a brown stone
she is a lavender blush
and I am a mauve to her flame

her past and her fuchsia
she is indigenous to indigo
and I am azure waves of grain

sweet orange and myrrh
she is the ultra violet
and I am Navy's aquamarine

sage woman chartreuse the man
in magenta fields opposites attract
where envy isn't all that is green

autumn even when the leaves turn
two amaranthine hearts crimson spoon
a total eclipse of the maroon

The Keeping Room

The grounds keeper is in
the keeping room waiting for
the water closet occupied by
the benefactor's daughter and
the haberdasher

the sous-chef is serving time in
the courtyard watching
the water clock because
the sundial is in use by
the chambermaid and
the letter carrier

the horologist is leaning against
the counter clockwise watching
the taxi dancer with
the hour glass Figure
making time stand still

Fills My Bucket

The things I have sensed
with this nose of mine
that sits below beautiful eyes
and above witted words
the stench of a granddaughter's diaper
the trash that I now treasure
the rain from Irene's reign
the stargazer lilies and the sunflowers
that have come to know the vase
adorning the corner of the desk well
leaving behind the aroma of love
the dust from the vacuum
that brought on a sneeze moments
before looking out of my office
window to see if it was you
that made the earthquake.

Signs of Rain

I am Dark Cloud of the Quechuan tribe
she is Forbidden Thunder
when she does her rain dance
I have to fight back the tears

Between Buttermilk Buns

Aisle
seven
the bread aisle
between buttermilk buns
that is where the misdemeanor
occurred prosecuted for shoplifting
your DNA was all over this crime scene
that is where a kiss was stole

The Pugilist

Standing in the corner
sparring with demons
so striking even when
the gloves came off
she was beautiful

refused to remain
trapped in a box
not throwing in the towel
in an undisputed prize
wanted a contender
to have a fighting chance
her desire for me
to go down on one knee
and to engage fisticuffs

Borrowed Wings

In a wheel chair by the window
sits an angel looking out onto the world
from her perch she imagines she can
abdicate her throne as I watch
she steals away celestial moments
because there is an affinity
I'm compelled to aid and abet
so as I fly away to far off places
bringing back pieces to share with her
and though these are places she cannot go
she waits stolen moments
to borrow my wings

The Ocean's Point Of View

A hand full of sand ice in the other
as time passes the sand will slip
through the cerulean gap and ice
in the other will melt
it is hard to hold a heart of sand
hard to hold when the heart is ice cold
in time it all slips away
so I'll have mine in a cup
with no ice on a beach with no sand
to slide into the ocean and be
washed away or to crash head first
into the heart of an iceberg
that eventually melts away
to be fastened to a heart
that is quick to sand to be
fastened to love that melts
is to be fastened to nothing at all
nothing sacred and secure

The Scenic Route

. . . And she said

come with me
as I journey the world

and while in Paris
I will tower for you

on our trip to London
I will tame the river

and on the third day
we will rise in Jerusalem

I your audience and Rome will ovation
the mezzanine level coliseum

just before taking your hand
to slow dance to the crack of the bells

after the climb we will
encore on the plateau

on the south side of Heaven
north of brotherly love

Baby's Breath

Do you notice the innocence
surrounding lily's ambition
the everlasting love
the regal celebration
do you feel drawn to the festivities
pure and sincere
eglantine and poetry in bloom
beautiful and the garnish
the window dressing
the baby's breath all goes unnoticed
accentuating lily and her scarlet curves
and crystal vase and her delivery
there is a melodic note in the key of
B sharp hanging in the air
and fingers dancing across the harp
lily uncultivated chaste
planted in the chapel
and soon invisible
her surname will become maiden

Lemon Serenade

She made her stand
her cup was half full
her complement
was not complimentary
she was charged a dime piece
beauty and charm
she planned to buy her way
into the starboard
the siren's
seductive and sultry
song was bitter sweet
just when I learned to tread water
she poured me the sailor
on to ice over the rocks
and now I am drowning
in here delicious voice

Before You Evanesce

I know that I do not visit often
that does not mean that I do not miss you.
I am the man that I am because of you.
you have helped to mold me.
it is because of you that I am fashioned this way.
when I am gifted with a compliment of
a mannered well or names are thrown
my way like gentleman or mid-knight,
you are the cause.
when she is smitten by my charm,
I thank you for the inheritance.
I remember Tioga and I remember you.
I remember Gratz and I remember you.
I remember Lehigh and I remember you.
I remember Wyalusing and I remember you.
I remember Diamond and I ' you.
indelible like her pen you are etched into my heart.
if today is prodigal and I appear to evanesce . . . .

then ' the morrow promises of my love.

Signals of Smoke and Ash

For me it was love at first sight

but she had the audacity to tell her girlfriend that I wasn't her type as if
I was O- and could not make her heart skip a beat now ever since the
doctor first pricked my heel and all the grade school I have been A+

for me it was love at first sight

she had the audacity to tell her sister that this ashy behind guy tried to
talk to her even when my mother would lick her finger to get that ashy
spot off my face or when she would cake my face in Vaseline even then
you could see my shine

for me it was love at first sight

and I hope that she does not let this ashiness cloud the windows of our
future a future in which I am contemplating getting down on one knee
getting it scuffed, scarred and ashy and I hope that she is not blinded by
this ashy knee that she can't see what is in my hand and I hope that she
is not blinded by this ashy hand that she cannot see what is in my heart

for me it was love

and I plan on making her my future making her my queen building her a castle brick by brick like a mason even if I have to work three jobs. I plan on building her a throne out of the finest woods like a carpenter getting these hands splintered scuffed, scarred and ashy. and with these arms and these hands I plan on holding her passionately and when these ashy lips kiss the middle they will ignite a fire inside of her that will burn for eternity's eternity and on the nights that she wants it rough well then these hands already come equipped I plan on holding her hand as I coach her through Lamaze as she gives birth to our son cutting the umbilical cord and getting up nights when he is crying and holding him and reading to him about his mother the queen. if you think that I am offering her a man that will worship her then you too are clouded by the ash. what I am offering her is a man that is not afraid of getting down on both knees getting them scuffed, scarred and ashy clasping these ashy hands together and worshiping with her

for me unconditional agape love

To Flavor with Grace

To one half of the twins
dearest sister of Larenz
to flavor is Father's wish
to see ancient the days
to do it with such grace
while holding the hand
of the one that birthed
never giving her release

The Messenger Bag

There is a courier
with love's manuscript
an emissary carrying
powerful words
on scrolls that are fragile
that must be handled with care
these words have a destiny
these words lead me
words that have been
seduced by the quill
dipped in her page
and I am in love
with the scribe
and she loves
to be read

Breakfast with D.E.L.L.A

Dearest everything,

    forever I want to wake

        with your sweet face

            lying next to mine.

                I want to have breakfast

                    with my darling everlasting,

                        my life my love my angel.

                            to greet each morning

                                just shy of Heaven

Tuesday in Mourning

There are some things that aren't
better than catching your death
there are some things better catching
there are some things better to be caught
Tuesday will never be the wiser

The Beginning of Her Happy Ending

On the ground she dropped
all of her cares and I bent to
pick them up and while I was
down on one knee I made
my proposal to fill the feel
of her to take all of her pain
away to be the healer of hurt
attentive to her every need
to reside in the chambers of
her heart forever the beginning
of her happy ending

A Breath of Fresh Heir

If you are
my breath
of fresh heir
my inherent
love is the
inherited
deposits in
your trust fund

Honey in Full Moon

The ceramic tiles on the floor
lily white and cool under my feet
the bed sheets unfurled across the bed
pearl white warm from heat
a dress eggshell white
running on the chaise so neat
on the balcony under the stars
incandescent white looking
like a constellation herself
is nectar and wild honey
in full moon

The Southside of Heaven

Come with me to the vineyard
Martha's namesake and like the
fermentation of grapes intoxicate
me with your words If not with
words then with photographs of you
because even the consumption of
your photo speaks volumes